MASTER MAP
WITH ORDNANCE SURVEY

Patricia Harrison
Steve Harrison

Contents

MAP MAKING
THEN AND NOW

Maps have been drawn and used for centuries. In 1574 Christopher Saxton began to produce County maps for the British Isles. The map on this page was drawn in 1577 and shows part of the County of Cheshire. Maps have become more accurate. The Ordnance Survey today uses high technology to produce modern maps.

Look at Saxton's map.

Draw the symbols Saxton used for

▶ water, hill, Castle (at Flint), tree, Church (at Chester), bridge.

Drawings in the sea were for decoration.

▶ How were ships powered in Saxton's time?
▶ What else has been drawn in the water?

In the sixteenth century an 's' in the middle of a word was written ∫. We have to be careful not to confuse this with an 'f', written ƒ .

Find the names of

▶ Three places which have an ∫ in the name.
▶ Three places which have an 'f' in the name.
▶ Write all six in the way Saxton did and then in modern writing.

This is the modern Ordnance Survey map of the same area.

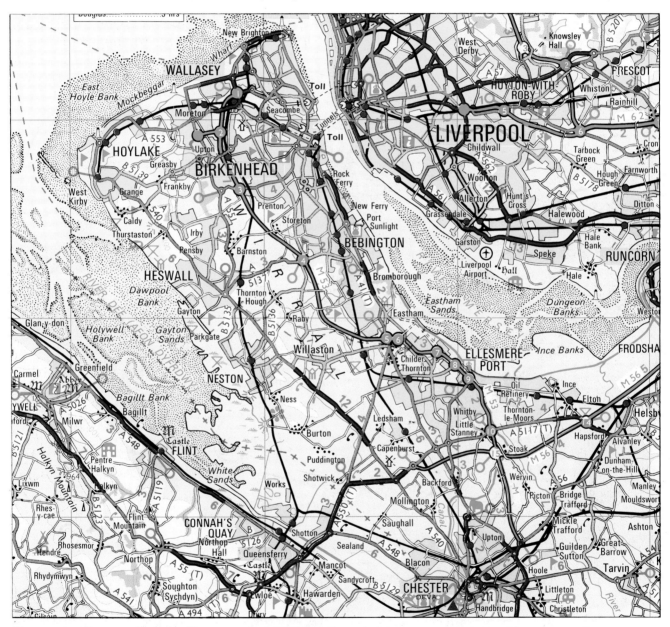

Compare the two maps. Copy and complete the chart.

SAXTON	ƒlu:			Wyrwir	We∫tkirkbye		FLYNT.	
O.S.		Picton	LIVERPOOL			Irby		WALLASEY

▶ What has happened to the River Dee since 1577?
▶ Why does only one map show railways and canals?

3

A BIRD'S EYE VIEW

Aerial photographs are used to make sure maps are accurate.

This one is part of Southampton.

The *map* shows the same area as the photograph.

▶ Copy and complete the chart.

Say which from the list can be seen only on the map, only on the photo, on both.

traffic,
street names,
containers,
water,
ships,
use of buildings,

football pitches,
railway line,
road numbers,
subways,
sewage works,
parking.

Aerial Photo	Map	Both
		Sewage Works

▶ Why are ships and traffic not shown on maps?

▶ Why do street names not appear on the photo?

By using the map and the photo we can see how the land is used.

We can divide the area into four main uses.

Housing. Leisure. Transport. Industry.

For each of these grid squares say how the land is used. One has been done for you.

▶ H5, C6, F7, E5, G6, A6, H4, F5, C1, E7.

LAND USE			
Housing	Leisure	Transport	Industry
		H5	

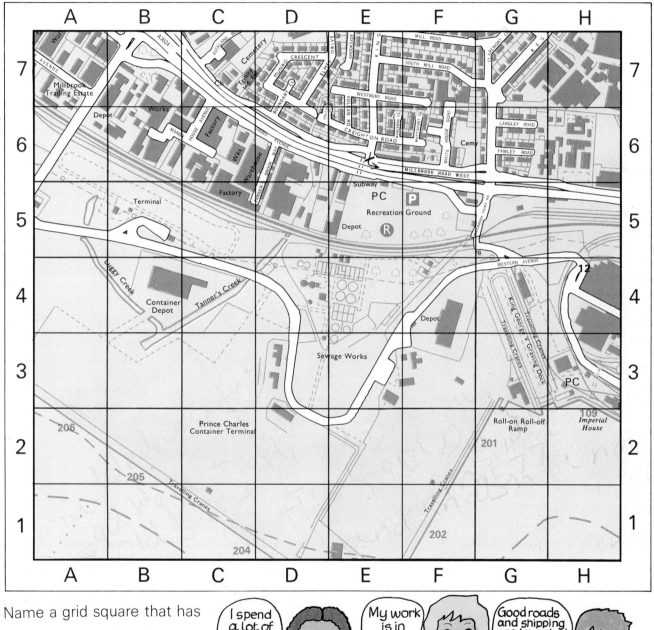

Name a grid square that has

▶ Industry and housing
▶ Leisure and industry
▶ Industry and transport
▶ List the grid squares in which containers are stored.

I spend a lot of time in F5

My work is in C7

Good roads and shipping are important to me H4 looks right

Match the people to the statements.

EXPLORING CAERNARFON CASTLE

Castles can be exciting places to visit. One of the finest in Europe is Caernarfon Castle in North Wales. Building started in 1283 and continued until 1330. A castle visit is much more interesting with the help of an aerial photo and a map.

When the English built castles in North Wales they often built towns next to them and protected the town with a wall.

Look at the aerial photograph.
▶ Which has the higher walls, the castle or the town?
▶ How many towers has the castle?

▶ Where would you feel safer if an attack came, in the castle or in the town. Why?
▶ How many gateways in the town walls can you see?
▶ Are most of the buildings inside the town wall newer or older than the wall itself?

Explain your answer.

▶ How many sides of the castle are flanked by water?
▶ Why was the castle built next to the water and not in the middle of the town?
▶ Describe what you can see on the far side of the bridge.
▶ Why do you think building took place next to the castle and not on the far side of the river?

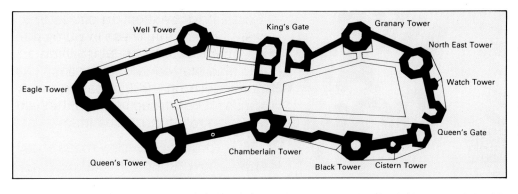

The castle plan gives the names of the towers.
The O.S. map is at the 1:2500 scale and shows the castle and the ancient town.

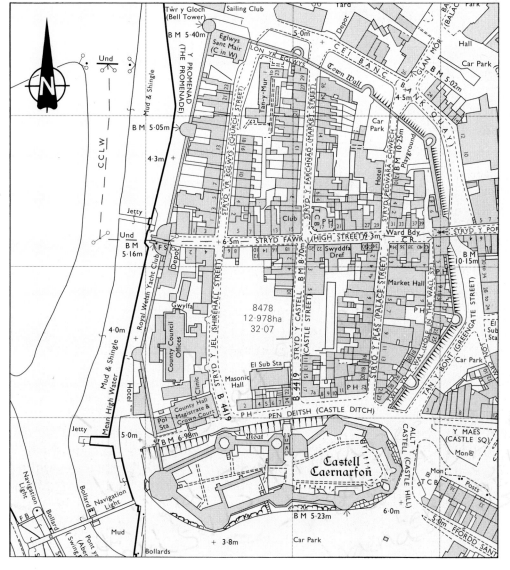

1. Suggest an activity that might have taken place in the
▶ Well Tower
▶ Granary Tower
▶ Watch Tower

2. Why is the map in two languages?

3. What is the Welsh for
▶ High Street
▶ Castle Ditch
▶ Bank Quay?

4. What is the English for
▶ Tan y Bont
▶ Allt y Castell
▶ Y Promenad?

5. On which street is the Police Station?

6. What is the Eglwys Sant Mair (clue, look at the name of the street).

Look at the plan, map and photo.

Say what you would see if you were standing
▶ on Eagle Tower looking South West
▶ on Chamberlain Tower looking South
▶ on Granary Tower looking North

Using Local Maps

Use OS mapping to locate the nearest castle to you.

▶ When was it built?
▶ Who built it?
▶ What is it built of?
▶ Why was it built?
▶ Compare it to Caernarfon Castle.

UPS AND DOWNS

If you visited the mountains what would you want to do? Climb a mountain, sail on a lake, walk along a valley? The skier in the picture did not check a map before setting off down the mountain.

Ordnance Survey maps show how steep the land is.

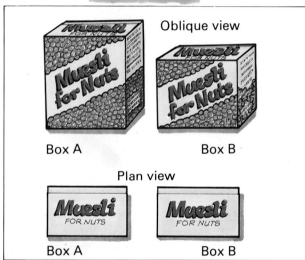

Oblique view

Box A   Box B

Plan view

Box A   Box B

▶ There is only one difference between the two boxes. What is it?
▶ Which view shows this difference best?

The problem is that a plan view does not show height. Look at the picture of the slide.

▶ How high is the slide?
▶ Which is steeper, the steps up or the slide down?
▶ How far apart are the steps?

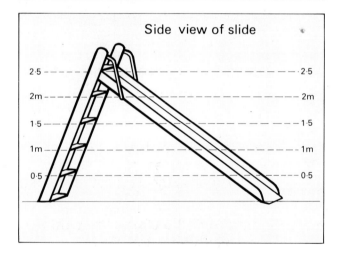

Side view of slide

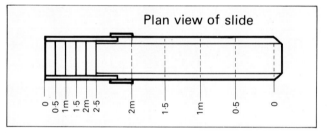

Plan view of slide

Look at the plan view of the slide.
To show the **difference** between the steepness of the steps and the slide, lines have been drawn showing height every 0·5m.
▶ Are the lines closer together on the steps or the slide?

Map makers use lines in the same way. Each line shows height. The closer together lines are the steeper the land. These lines are called **contour lines.**

Look at the map extract. The heights are given in feet.

▶ Does this show flat ground or hilly ground? How can you tell?

▶ How high is
(a) Great Gable?
(b) Kirk Fell?

▶ How many peaks has Kirk Fell?

Map A

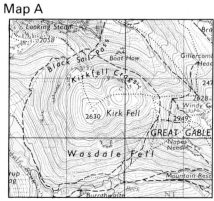

A valley is an area of land lower than the land around it.

Streams or rivers often run along valleys.

Map B shows a valley in the Lake District.
▶ What is the name of the stream running along the valley?
▶ What is the highest point
(a) West of the valley? (b) East of the valley?
▶ Why are roads usually built along valleys rather than over the peaks?

The valley is wide between Burn's Farm and Birkett Mire.

The valley is narrow between Low Bridgend and Fornside.

▶ Is the valley narrow or wide between
(a) Birkett Bank and Shundraw?
(b) Smaithwaite and Mill?
(c) Bridge House and Hilltop?

▶ If you were stood at Bramcrag to the east you would see a very steep slope (contour lines close together) to the west you would see the B5322, beyond the road St. John's Beck, the valley bottom and in the distance High Rigg.

▶ Describe what you would see if you were stood at
(a) Mire Ho   (b) Bridge Ho   (c) The top of Great How.

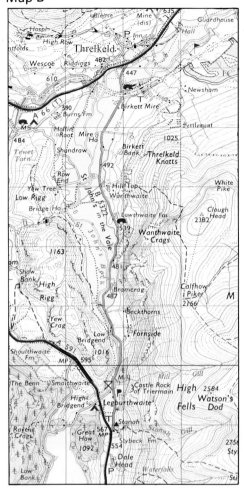

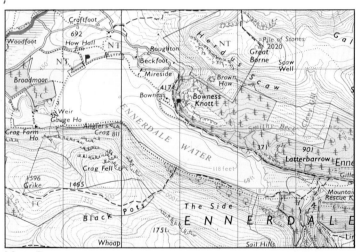

Map C

Maps use special contour lines to tell us about the depth of lakes.

Map C shows Ennerdale Water (depths are in feet).
▶ What depth is shown by the blue contour line nearest to the shore?
▶ How deep is the deepest part of the lake?

Remember: the closer the contour lines the steeper the slope.

▶ If you followed the path down from Black Pots and entered the lake would the slope be gentle or steep?
▶ If you entered the lake from How Hall Farm would it be gentle or steep?

▶ Match this photograph to one of Map A, B or C. Give your reasons.

Before visiting an area like the Lake District it is useful to obtain an O.S. map. As you travel along valleys use your map. Identify the mountains, hills, rivers and lakes around you.

Ben and Emma are spending five days in North Wales with their Mum, Sue. All three have different interests. They are using a map to plan visits from their youth hostel in Capel Curig.

EXPLORING NORTH WALES

The family used the map on the opposite page.
▶ Draw the symbols Ben, Emma and Sue will look for.
▶ Name four towns where Sue can visit castles.
▶ Name a mountain with a railway running to the summit.
▶ Name three locations where Ben could enjoy a picnic and a walk.
▶ Which town has a steam railway, a castle and a picnic area close by?

Emma wanted to know what the Welsh place names mean. By investigating the map she was able to discover some meanings for herself. She tried to match the words with local physical features.
▶ Use the map to match the four Welsh words to their English equivalents.
Llyn, Port(h), Afon, Pen, *Hill, River, Harbour, Lake.*
▶ If the family saw this sign **Traeth** what could they do there?

Ben and Emma enjoy directing Sue to mystery destinations. They sit in the back and give careful directions, which Sue follows.

Read the directions they gave and identify the destination.

▶ Now write the route descriptions for Sue to follow from Capel Curig to:
(a) Beaumaris
(b) Blaenau Ffestiniog
(c) Beddgelert
(d) Caernarfon

Take the A5 North West from Capel Curig. Pass Llyn Ogwen on the right. Follow the A5 to the junction with the A55. Turn right and drive along the Dual carriageway North East until you reach Conwy. Cross the river and turn right. Take the A470. Stop at the first railway station.

When planning visits it is important to work out how far you will travel and how long it will take. Emma uses a piece of string, which she lays along the route. The string is then measured against the map scale and the distance calculated.

Sue drives at about 60 km an hour in Wales, so they can also calculate the time a journey will take.

Using Local Maps

Imagine you will soon have visitors from another part of the country. Use the O.S. map for your area to plan:
(a) places to visit
(b) routes to follow
(c) time/distance charts for five days

▶ Copy and complete this chart.

From	To	Distance	Time	Purpose
Capel Curig	Bangor	30 km	30 mins	Swimming baths
Beddgelert				Caernarfon Castle
Criccieth				Steam train to Blaenau
Conwy	Betws-y-Coed			
Capel Curig	Llanberis			
Ffestiniog				Trawsfynydd Power Station

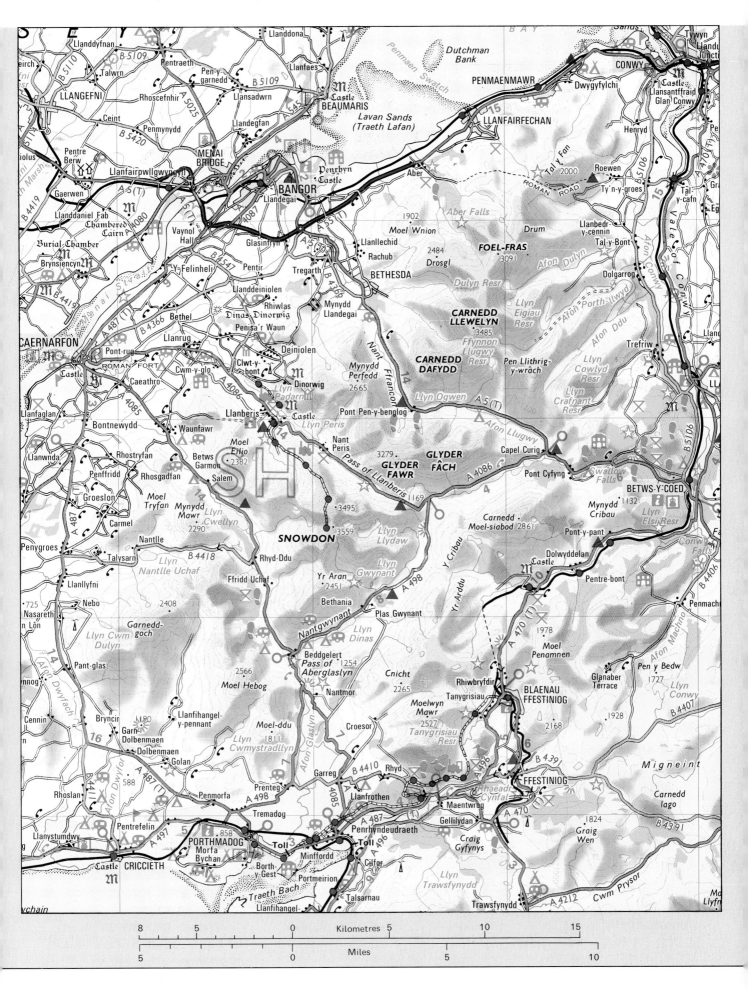

CENTRE SHOPPING

This Shopping Centre plan shows the Ealing Broadway Centre. It is drawn by *Goad Plans* who use the Ordnance Survey 1:1250 map as their starting point. *Goad Plans* produce plans for shopping centres in many parts of Britain and Europe.

THE EALING
BROADWAY CENTRE

▷ Match the six abbreviations to their definitions:

FT/WR	Vacant
L/FASH	Clothes
CLO	Confectioner
LEATH GDS	Ladies fashion
VAC	Footwear
CONF	Cosmetics
COS	Leather goods

▷ What do these abbreviations stand for:
JWLR, M/WR, L/WR, SHWRM, LAVS, CHEM, SMKT?

Which shops would you find at
▷ The Mall nos. 78, 61, 29, 55?
▷ What does each shop sell?
▷ How many sites are vacant? Dixons is a double unit. It is no. 65 so there is not a 66.

How many units are occupied by:
▷ Solo?
▷ Chelsea Man and Girl?
▷ Curry's?
▷ Safeways?
▷ What is the evidence on the plan that tells you there is more than one storey?

Use 1-cm squared paper to copy and complete the crossword.
Use the plan to help you.

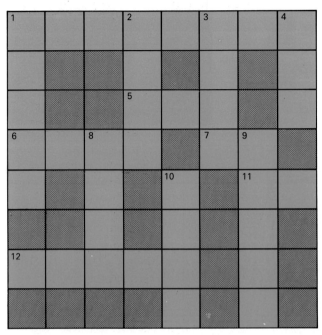

Answers on page 32.

Clues Across

1. Way In
5. One more than Dolcis
6. Where would the 'Pidgeons' lay their eggs?
7. Curry's sell it
11. Entrance
12. Take your prescription here

Clues Down

1. At Unit 75
2. Where Oliver puts his feet up
3. Shop after this one
4. You cannot do this with 'American Pie'
8. Flying alone
9. Have you got it taped?
10. _ _ _ _ Selfridge

Shoppers need to decide how good a Centre is. One way of doing this is to give marks for what the centre provides.

If you walked through a centre where most of the shops were vacant you would feel you had wasted your time, so you might give two marks out of ten. If most were full you might give eight marks out of ten.

▶ Use a scale of 1 to 10 for the Ealing Centre.

FACTOR	SCALE
Vacant shops:	All vacant 1. All full 10.
Traffic:	Heavy traffic 1. No traffic 10.
Weather:	Completely open 1. Sheltered 10.
Choice:	All shops the same 1. Variety of shops 10.

▶ Do the same for a shopping centre near you.
▶ You can add other factors such as:

Litter:	Filthy 1. Clean 10.
Movement:	Steep steps 1. Escalators/lifts 10.
Car Park:	Far away 1. On same site 10.

Some factors make people disagree.
What scores would you give for:
▶ Music?
▶ No children allowed without adults?
▶ Artificial lights
▶ Street musicians (buskers)
▶ Charity collections
Ask others to find if they agree.

Old dock areas in many parts of Britain are now being given a new life. One of the biggest projects is the *Albert Dock* in *Liverpool*.

The dock was opened in 1846 by Prince Albert. Liverpool was one of the greatest ports in the world. Today a new use has been found for the docks.

THE ALBERT DOCK

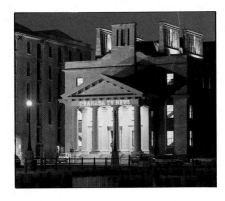

To understand the changes that have taken place an old Ordnance Survey map is a great help.

▶ How many buildings are part of the Maritime Museum?

Where would you go if you wanted to
▶ see a famous painting
▶ shop
▶ show your parents where to buy a 'pint'
▶ learn about the history of the sea?

Now use the 1893 O.S. map to help you. What were the following buildings used for in 1893?
▶ T.V. Studio
▶ Tate Gallery
▶ Atlantic Pavillion
▶ The Maritime Museum North of Canning Half-tide dock.

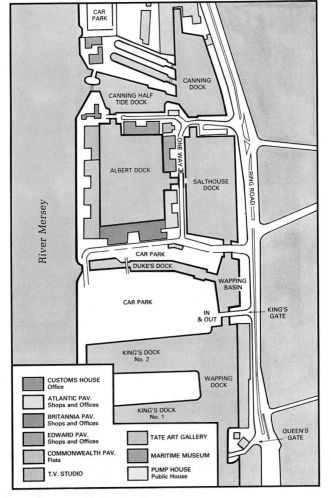

CAR PARK
CANNING DOCK
CANNING HALF TIDE DOCK
ONE WAY
ALBERT DOCK
SALTHOUSE DOCK
River Mersey
RING ROAD
CAR PARK
DUKE'S DOCK
WAPPING BASIN
CAR PARK
IN & OUT
KING'S GATE
KING'S DOCK No. 2
WAPPING DOCK
CUSTOMS HOUSE Office
ATLANTIC PAV. Shops and Offices
BRITANNIA PAV. Shops and Offices
EDWARD PAV. Shops and Offices
COMMONWEALTH PAV. Flats
T.V. STUDIO
KING'S DOCK No. 1
TATE ART GALLERY
MARITIME MUSEUM
PUMP HOUSE Public House
QUEEN'S GATE

▶ Name three buildings that stood where the largest car park is now.

Imagine you had entered the lock at Duke's Dock from the Mersey in 1893. You sailed through the docks to re-enter the river at Canning Island:
▶ List the docks you passed through.
▶ How many bridges would have been opened for you?
▶ Compare the layout of Wapping Dock and King's Dock in 1893 and today. Describe the changes.

Many goods were imported and exported through these docks. Use the 1893 map to find evidence of which goods. Copy and complete the chart.

EVIDENCE	LOCATION	GOODS
Timber Yard	Tabley St.	Wood
		Tobacco
	Beckwith St.	
Sugar Works		
	N. of King's Dock	
		Soap
Canning Foundry		
Bonded Warehouse		

▶ Look at the three photos on this page.
Match each photo with one of these three locations from 1893: Albert Dock Offices, Warehouse N, Warehouse E.

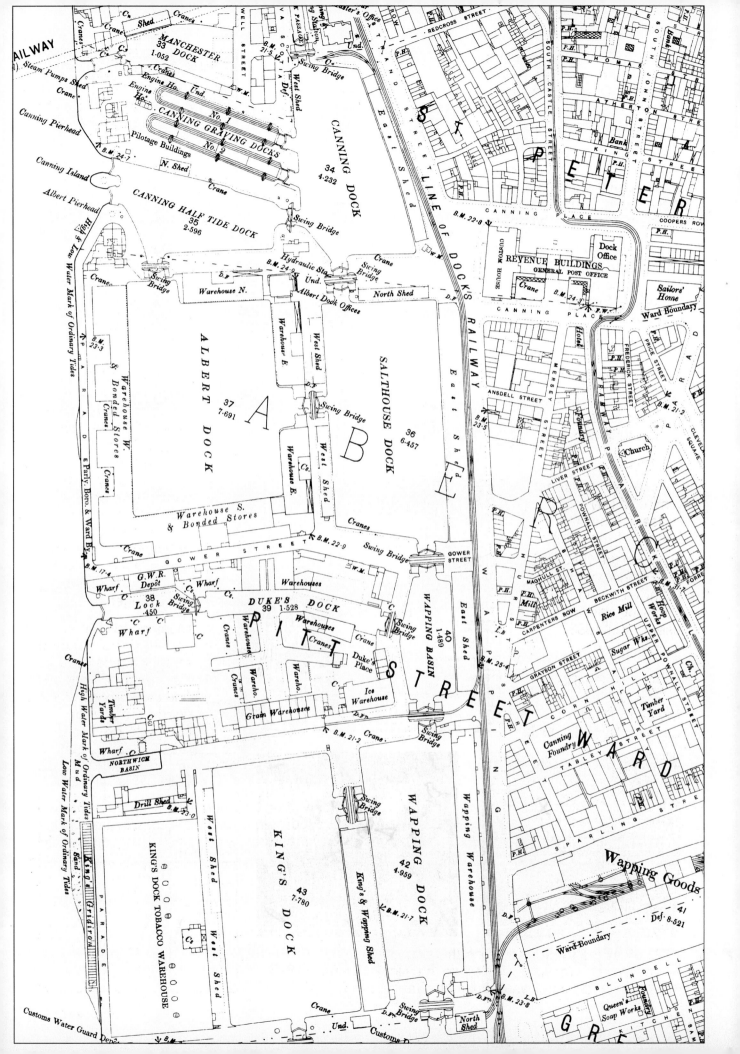

CLUES TO THE PAST

A mountain top is not the best site for a village! Villages and towns have grown in their present locations for good reasons.

A

Rivers were an obstacle to travellers. One solution was to build a bridge.

▶ Why has the bridge been built at this point?
▶ Why do road builders then bring roads to this location?
▶ Why would these buildings have been useful when the village first began?

B

When danger threatened people would hurry to shelter in a *fortified* building defended by a moat. The safest place to erect other buildings was near the moat.

▶ How did a moat act as a defence?
▶ How did friendly visitors cross?

C

When two roads met they brought travellers together. Such people might rest, sleep, trade, talk. A crossroads soon had a number of buildings built close by and a new village was under way.

▶ Which feature tells you that traders came here?
▶ Why do many old inns have stables attached?

D

Many people earned their living from the sea. Only some sites along the coast were suitable for harbours.

▶ Which of these features would you look for in choosing a harbour:
deep water; exposed; shallow water; jagged rocks; shelter; on a headland; in a bay?
▶ Which of these jobs depend on the sea: farmer, sailor, miner, fisher, ferryperson, coastguard, shepherd, lighthouse keeper, weaver, sailmaker?

MAP A

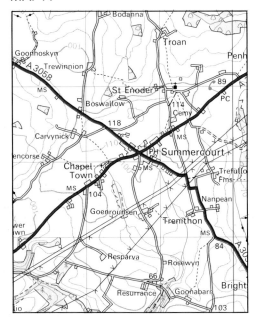

We can use modern Ordnance Survey Maps to search for clues to the past. The four map extracts on this page tell us something about our history.

MAP B

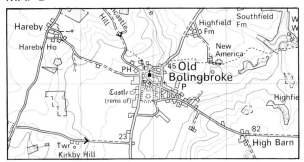

▶ Match the following descriptions to two of the map extracts.

1 This village is built around the remains of a castle. Roads run on all sides of the castle. House building has followed the line of the roads. This village was a *fortified* site in the past.

2 There are two towns in this map extract. Both are ports. They are in bays where there is shelter. Both have lighthouses close by. The towns have gradually grown inland as time has passed. These villages were probably fishing ports in the past.

▶ Now write descriptions for the other two map extracts. Say why you think these settlements may have first been built.

MAP C

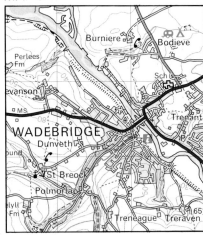

▶ Which settlements have names that give us clues to the past?
▶ Which two of the settlements try to attract tourists?
▶ Why are there lighthouses in the sea near Penzance and Newlyn?

Using Local Maps

Choose a local village or town and look for clues to its past — Why do you think it developed in this place?
▶ You can do the same when you visit other parts of Britain on holiday. Be a holiday detective by using a map of the area.

MAP D

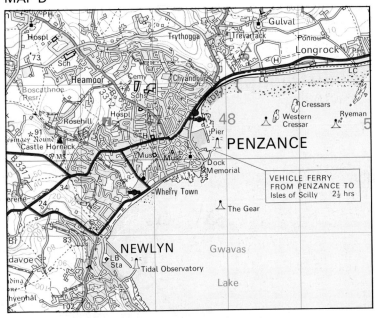

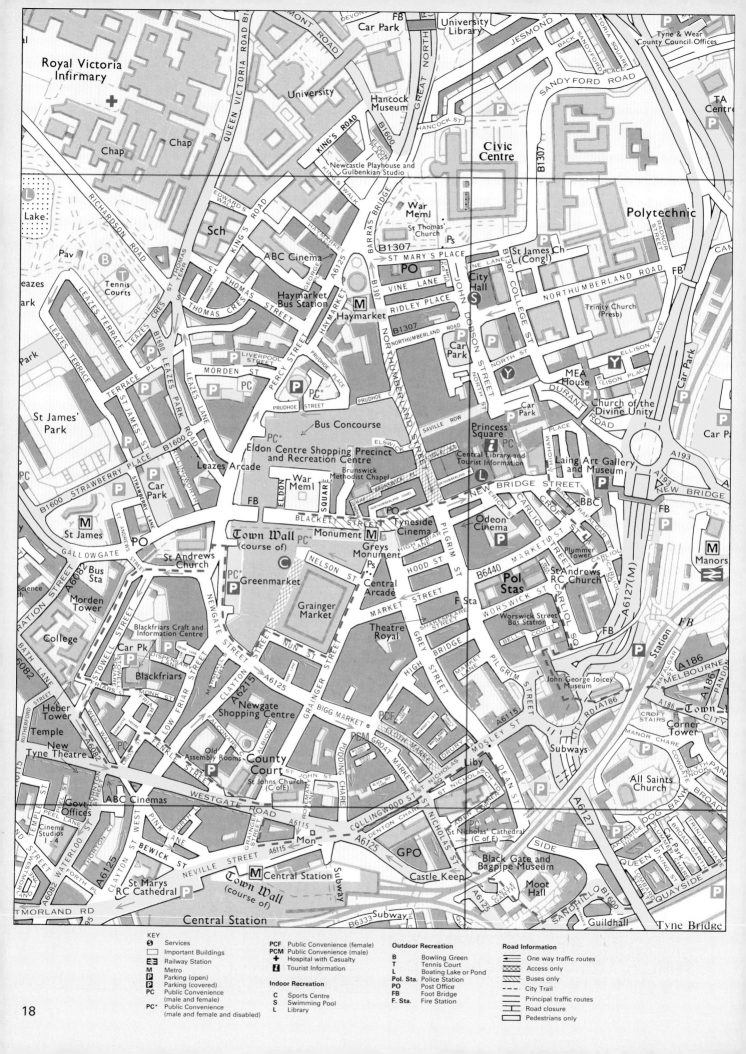

KEY

S Services
☐ Important Buildings
≋ Railway Station
M Metro
P Parking (open)
P Parking (covered)
PC Public Convenience (male and female)
PC* Public Convenience (male and female and disabled)

PCF Public Convenience (female)
PCM Public Convenience (male)
+ Hospital with Casualty
∄ Tourist Information

Indoor Recreation

C Sports Centre
S Swimming Pool
L Library

Outdoor Recreation

B Bowling Green
T Tennis Court
L Boating Lake or Pond
Pol. Sta. Police Station
PO Post Office
FB Foot Bridge
F. Sta. Fire Station

Road Information

⇒ One way traffic routes
▨ Access only
▧ Buses only
--- City Trail
▬ Principal traffic routes
☐ Road closure
☐ Pedestrians only

The Blyth family decided to spend the day visiting Newcatle upon Tyne. Mrs Blyth said they should plan the day carefully in order to get the most out of their visit. She bought a city map of Newcastle and the planning began.

A DAY IN THE CITY

All the family listed the things they would like to do in Newcastle. Mr Blyth said he wanted to see some paintings. He checked the map and the key and found the Laing Art Gallery. He wrote down

Activity	Place	Location
View paintings	Laing Art Gallery	Higham Place

▶ Complete the chart for the rest of the family. Say what activity they did and the location of each of the places visited: museum, town wall, sports centre, theatre, shopping precinct, market, swimming pool, university, lake.

Mrs Blyth drove into Newcastle across the Tyne Bridge. The rest of the family worked out her route through the city.

TASK Follow these directions and name the Blyth's destinations.
▶ North along the A6127. Carry on along Pilgrim St past the fire station. Turn east down Newbridge St and park at the end of the street. Which of the places in the list did they visit?
▶ Leave the car park. Drive south past the BBC into Market St. At the crossroads with Grey St turn south. Your destination is on the left in Shakespeare St.

Now plan your own routes between the following locations. Pay careful attention to the one-way system and other road rules.
▶ From the Theatre Royal to St Nicholas' Cathedral
▶ St Nicholas' Cathedral to St James' Park (football ground)
▶ St James' Park to the Polytechnic

Mr Blyth liked Newcastle because it had facilities for the disabled.
▶ Name two locations where toilets suitable for Mr Blyth are provided.

Look at the four pictures. Use the map and say
▶ Where the event is taking place.
▶ How you would reach there by car from the Tyne Bridge.

Newcastle has a very modern metro system.

▶ Name three roads the metro passes under on its journey from St James to Manors.
▶ Name the two cinemas it passes under.
▶ Which is the nearest metro station to:

Tyne Bridge?
Grainger Market?
St James' Park football ground?

HISTORY TRAIL

Have you ever wondered what your local town was like 100 years ago? You can investigate how much a town has changed by comparing a modern map with an old map.

Look carefully at Maps A and B. One is modern, the other shows the area 100 years ago.

▷ Which map is modern? Give three pieces of evidence for your choice.
▷ Which map is 100 years old?
Give two pieces of evidence.
▷ How many buildings can you find which are used for the same purpose on both maps?
▷ Name three buildings which have disappeared from the old map? What has taken their place?

The names of roads can often give clues to what happened there in the past.

▷ Match these four clues with four roads on the map.

(a) A stream called 'The Skye' once ran along here.

(b) Cock fighting was a popular sport along this street.

(c) A spring of water *spurted* up here and was carried up the narrow main street.

(d) Towards the river there stood a gate in medieval times.

Map A

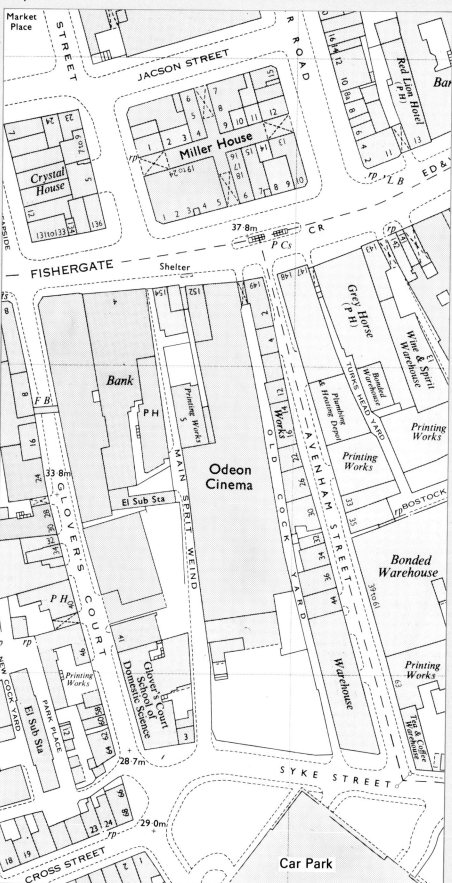

Map B

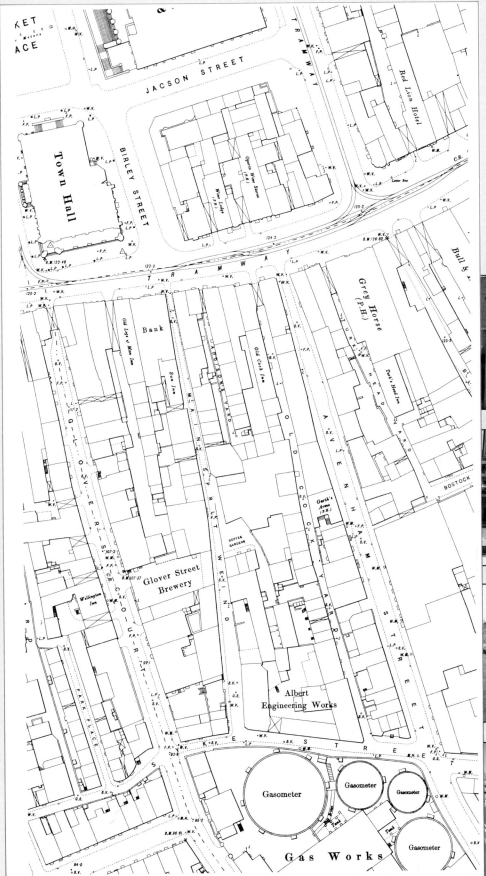

Look carefully at the photographs.

Copy and complete the charts.

Present day		
Photo	Name	Street
A	Odeon cinema	Fishergate
B		
C		

100 years ago	
A	Many small buildings
B	
C	

Photograph A

Photograph B

Photograph C

Photograph D

London is so busy that the only way people can move quickly is to travel underground.

Beneath the streets there is a whole railway system. A visitor to London needs a map of the *underground* or they might never arrive at their destination.

MOVING AROUND LONDON

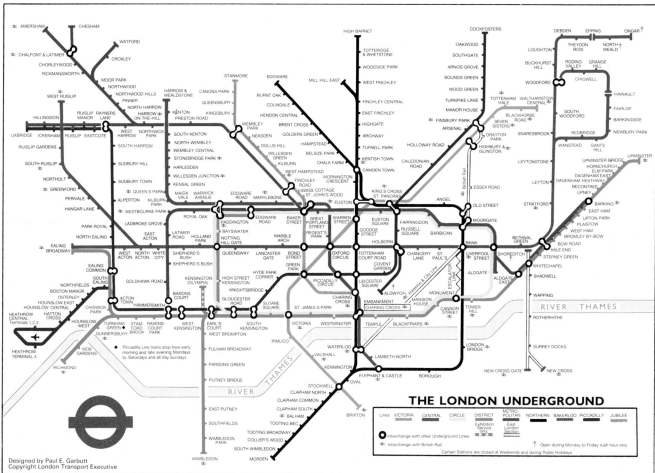

Designed by Paul E. Garbutt
Copyright London Transport Executive

Using the Map

Each route, or *line,* has a name and a colour.

If you want to travel from Liverpool St to Westminster the map shows that you need the yellow route. This is the *Circle* line.

Which lines would you follow to travel
▶ from Earl's Court to Wimbledon?
▶ from Oxford Circus to St Paul's?
▶ from Marylebone to Piccadilly Circus?
▶ from Waterloo to Tottenham Court Rd?
▶ Name the stations you would pass through on each journey.

Sometimes your journey will not be so simple. You may have to change trains. You can change at stations that are shown with this symbol

▶ Copy and complete the chart showing journeys that need a change. The first one has been done for you. There may be more than one correct answer.

START		CHANGE		DESTINATION
Place	Line	Place	Line	
Marble Arch	Central	Bond St.	Jubilee	Baker St.
Queensbury				Preston Road
Stratford				Upminster
Wimbledon				Covent Garden

Now write out your own start and destination stations and try them on a friend.

Visitors to London who want to visit a theatre or cinema use a map that features places of entertainment. Use the map and key together.

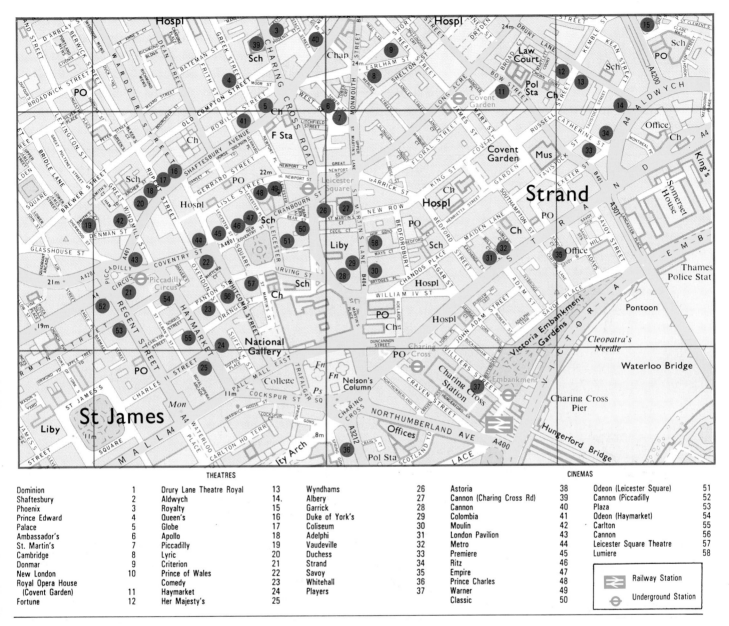

THEATRES							
Dominion	1	Drury Lane Theatre Royal	13	Wyndhams	26	Astoria	38
Shaftesbury	2	Aldwych	14	Albery	27	Cannon (Charing Cross Rd)	39
Phoenix	3	Royalty	15	Garrick	28	Cannon	40
Prince Edward	4	Queen's	16	Duke of York's	29	Colombia	41
Palace	5	Globe	17	Coliseum	30	Moulin	42
Ambassador's	6	Apollo	18	Adelphi	31	London Pavilion	43
St. Martin's	7	Piccadilly	19	Vaudeville	32	Metro	44
Cambridge	8	Lyric	20	Duchess	33	Premiere	45
Donmar	9	Criterion	21	Strand	34	Ritz	46
New London	10	Prince of Wales	22	Savoy	35	Empire	47
Royal Opera House		Comedy	23	Whitehall	36	Prince Charles	48
(Covent Garden)	11	Haymarket	24	Players	37	Warner	49
Fortune	12	Her Majesty's	25			Classic	50

CINEMAS	
Odeon (Leicester Square)	51
Cannon (Piccadilly)	52
Plaza	53
Odeon (Haymarket)	54
Carlton	55
Cannon	56
Leicester Square Theatre	57
Lumiere	58

Railway Station
Underground Station

▶ What are the names of cinemas 45, 53, 55, 42?

▶ In which roads do these four cinemas stand?

▶ What are the names of theatres 24, 14, 16, 25?

▶ In which roads do these theatres stand?

▶ Which cinemas are next to:
(a) The Coliseum Theatre?
(b) Piccadilly Circus Underground Station?

▶ Which theatres are next to:
(a) Charing Cross Station?
(b) Covent Garden Underground Station?

▶ If you start at the 'Empire' Cinema and travel west, which four cinemas will you pass on the way to Piccadilly Circus?

Now use the 'entertainments' map and the 'underground' map together.

Copy and complete the chart for the five underground stations on the map. The first one has been done for you.

Underground Station	Lines	Nearest Cinema	Nearest Theatre
Embankment	Circle: District: Northern: Bakerloo	Lumiere	Players
Charing Cross			
Piccadilly Circus			
Leicester Sq.			
Covent Garden			

SUPER SUMMERS

Every summer millions of people head for the holiday resorts. Holiday makers need a special type of map — one which will show them how to get the most from a summer holiday. The Ordnance Survey's 'Holiday Map and Guide' series provides detailed holiday information for visitors.

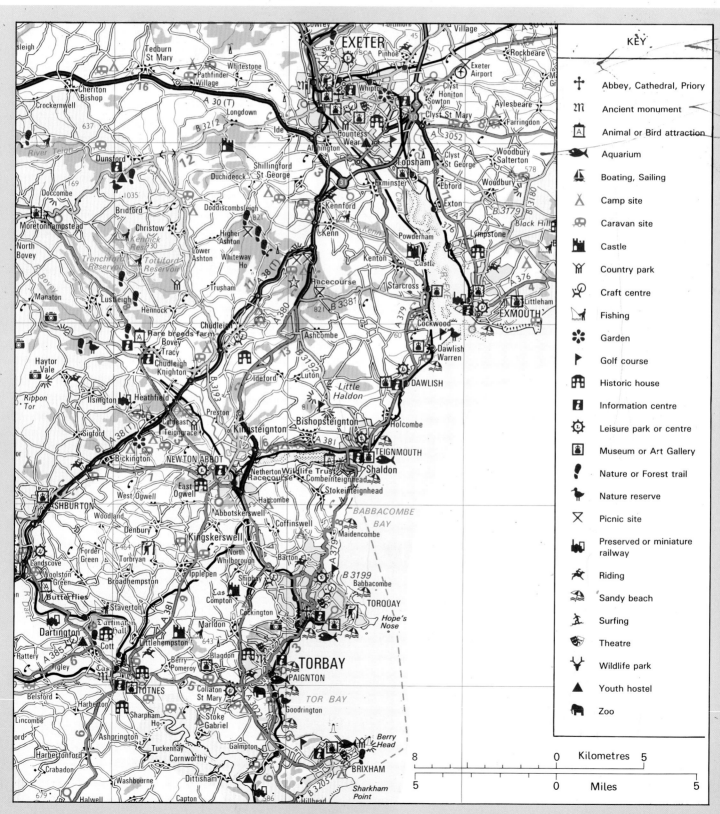

KEY

☩	Abbey, Cathedral, Priory
ᛗ	Ancient monument
Ⓐ	Animal or Bird attraction
🐟	Aquarium
⛵	Boating, Sailing
🏕	Camp site
🚐	Caravan site
🏰	Castle
🌲	Country park
🎨	Craft centre
🎣	Fishing
✳	Garden
⚑	Golf course
🏛	Historic house
ℹ	Information centre
⚙	Leisure park or centre
🖼	Museum or Art Gallery
👣	Nature or Forest trail
🦆	Nature reserve
✕	Picnic site
🚂	Preserved or miniature railway
🏇	Riding
🏖	Sandy beach
🏄	Surfing
🎭	Theatre
⚕	Wildlife park
▲	Youth hostel
🐘	Zoo

Kilometres
Miles

► Name three places where you can
(a) Find information about the area.
(b) Build sandcastles.
(c) Visit the theatre.

People visit the area for many reasons.

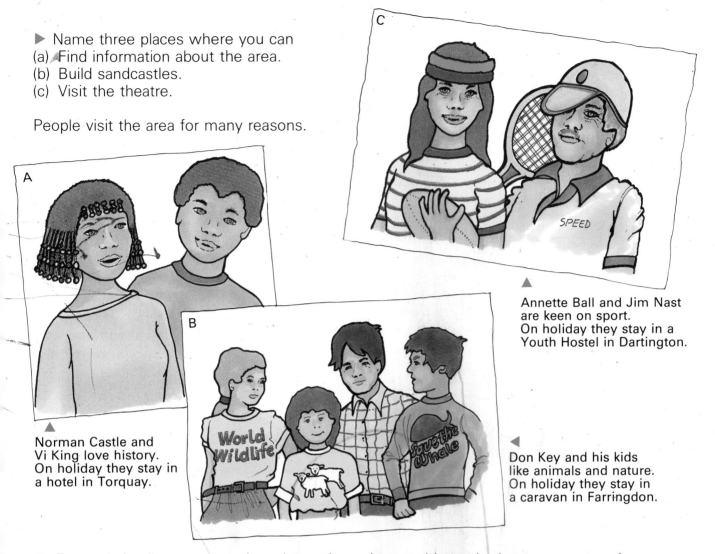

C

A

▲
Norman Castle and
Vi King love history.
On holiday they stay in
a hotel in Torquay.

B

▲
Annette Ball and Jim Nast
are keen on sport.
On holiday they stay in a
Youth Hostel in Dartington.

◄
Don Key and his kids
like animals and nature.
On holiday they stay in
a caravan in Farringdon.

► For each family, name another place where they could stay in the correct type of accommodation.

Here is a list of the activities they enjoyed. Copy and complete the chart. One has been done for you.

Horse riding
Visit a zoo
Squash at a leisure centre
Follow nature trail
See a stream train

Visit a castle
Visit a cathedral
Visit a wildlife park
Play golf
Tour an historic house

Bird watching
Sailing
Visit a museum
Go swimming
See rare farm animals

Activity	Symbol	Family	Location of Activity	Distance from place where family is staying
Riding	🐎	C	Totnes	5 km approx
Visit a Zoo				

List the six activities you would like to do if you visited the area. Write where you could find the activity and then choose a sensible location to stay.

MOUNTAIN RESCUE

EQUIPMENT

Walking Clothes
Walking boots
Waterproofs
Compass
Whistle
Food for day and
Emergency rations
Tent
Stove
Pans
Sleeping bags
Torch and batteries
Map
_____
Total weight of rucksack
11 kg

At 11 a.m. on a Saturday morning in early March three scouts set off from Limefitt Campsite, Troutbeck (417,032). They planned to meet their scout leader at the end of the lake (469,107) at 4 p.m.

The list shows what equipment the scouts took with them.

For each item on the list

▶ Write what it would be used for.
▶ Describe three possible emergencies which might happen when walking in the mountains.
▶ What would you include as emergency rations? Remember to think about weight.

The scouts did not arrive on time. A Mountain Rescue team began to search but could not find them in the mist. At 10 p.m. one of the scouts arrived back, cold and wet. He gave a report to the rescue team.

A

B

C

D

Report

11.30 We walked along track to Thornthwaite Crag following the old Roman Road.
1.30   We had lunch by the beacon.
1.50   Walked North East to High Street summit (height 2719ft.) at 2.40. Wind was blowing hard.
2.50   Set off S.E. towards Nan Bield Pass. Mist got worse, we felt cold.

We missed our way. Snow on the ground. John slipped and we think he has broken his leg.

We were cold, damp and it grew dark. We pitched a tent wrapped John up. Faruq stayed with him and I came for help.

I think we were just S.W. of Blea Water but I'm not sure.

E

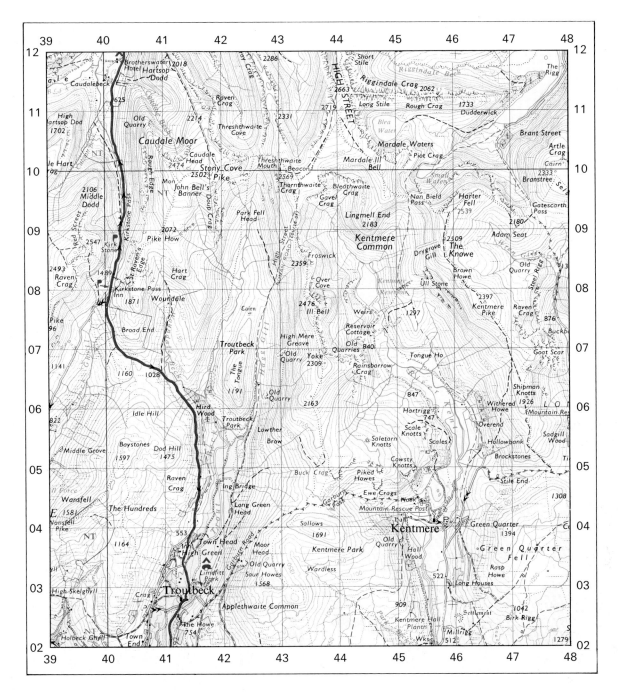

▶ Use your finger to follow the route the scouts took.

▶ Copy and complete the chart. One has been done for you.

Picture	Event	Grid Ref.
A	Set off	417,032
B		
C		
D		
E		

Kendal Mountain Rescue Team set off from Kentmere (458,040) at 7 a.m. the next day.

▶ Copy and complete their report.

We walked east and crossed the River ＿＿＿＿
We walked N ＿＿＿＿ along the v ＿＿＿＿＿. We
left the valley at T ＿＿＿＿＿ H ＿. As we walked
up we saw Kentmere R ＿＿＿＿＿＿＿＿ to the
W ＿＿＿. We followed the path to N ＿＿ B ＿＿＿＿
Pass. We walked N ＿＿＿＿ W ＿＿＿ until we
found the boys just S ＿＿＿＿ W ＿＿＿ of B ＿＿＿
W ＿＿＿＿.

BURIED TREASURE

One of the last pirates on the South Coast was a relative of Long John Silver — he was known as Short Jack Brass. Just before he died Jack buried his treasure and put a message in his favourite Dandelion & Burdock bottle. Soon afterwards he died when his wife fell on him.

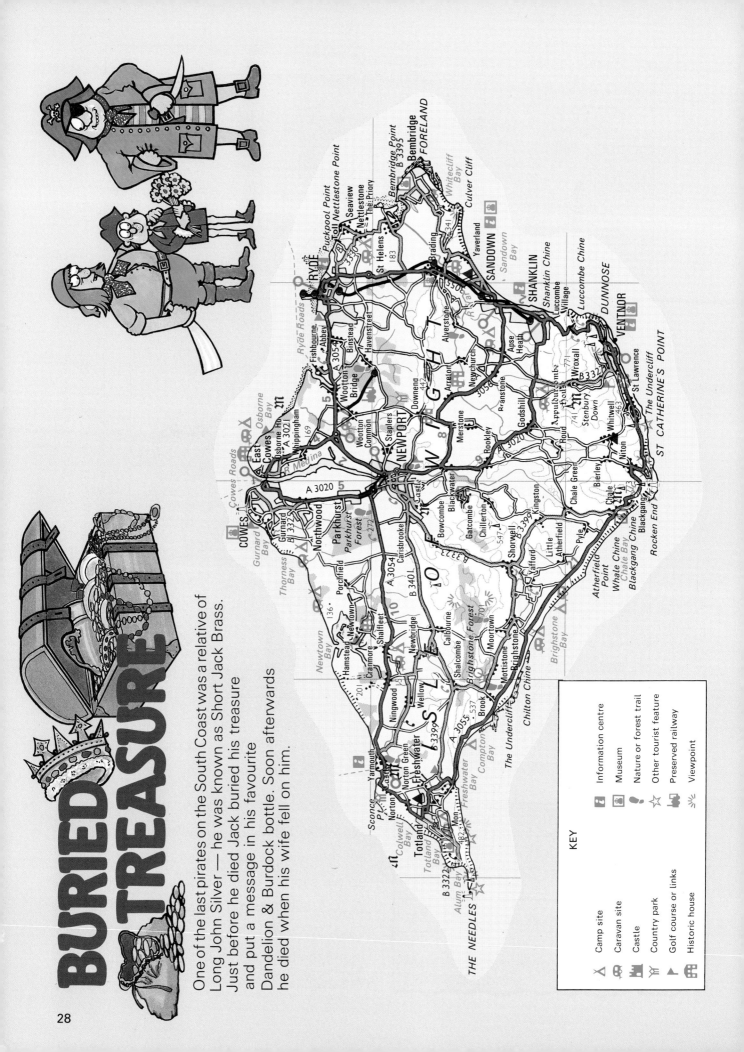

KEY

🅖 Information centre	
🏛 Museum	
🐾 Nature or forest trail	
☆ Other tourist feature	
🚂 Preserved railway	
🔆 Viewpoint	

⛺ Camp site	
🚐 Caravan site	
🏰 Castle	
🏕 Country park	
▲ Golf course or links	
🏚 Historic house	

Sandy Beach and her brother Rocky found the bottle whilst on holiday in the Isle of Wight. Inside they found the message still clear enough to read.

Jack was afraid his mother and his wife would steal his treasure so he wrote his messages in code.

There were four sets of instructions to follow. Each one would lead to a place on the island.

The treasure hidden at each place is contained within the name but sometimes the letters may need to be re-arranged. Two of the treasures are expensive minerals. Two are cheaper minerals.

Follow Jack's directions and write the message in full.

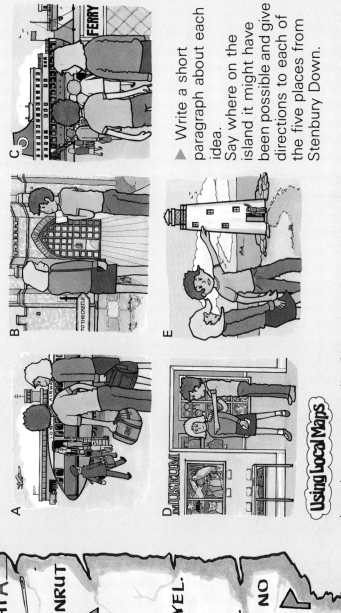

1 TRATS TA TSAE (MOO) OG S
GNOLA EHT A3021. SSAP
TA EHT NRUT E GNOLA EHT A
HGUORHT OT LOOPKCUP

2 LEVART S GNOLA EHT A ___ NRUT
W TA SSAP EHT
POTS TA NARB .

3 EUNITNOC ON A ___ OT
NRUT S HGUORHT YEL.
POTS TA SDOG

4 OG NO GNOLA EHT A ___
SSAP NRUT S TA ON
B___ POTS EROFEB EHT
TA NETS

▲ Choose four other locations on the Isle of Wight and write instructions like Jack's. Try them out on a friend.

Rocky and Sandy thought for a long time about what to do with the treasure. The five pictures show the ideas they considered.

▲ Write a short paragraph about each idea.
Say where on the island it might have been possible and give directions to each of the five places from Stenbury Down.

Using Local Maps

Imagine someone like Short Jack Brass lived in your area. Use a local map and make up instructions for your friends. Try to think of funny pictures to take the place of town names.

Answers on page 32.

Ordnance Survey

CONVENTIONAL SIGNS

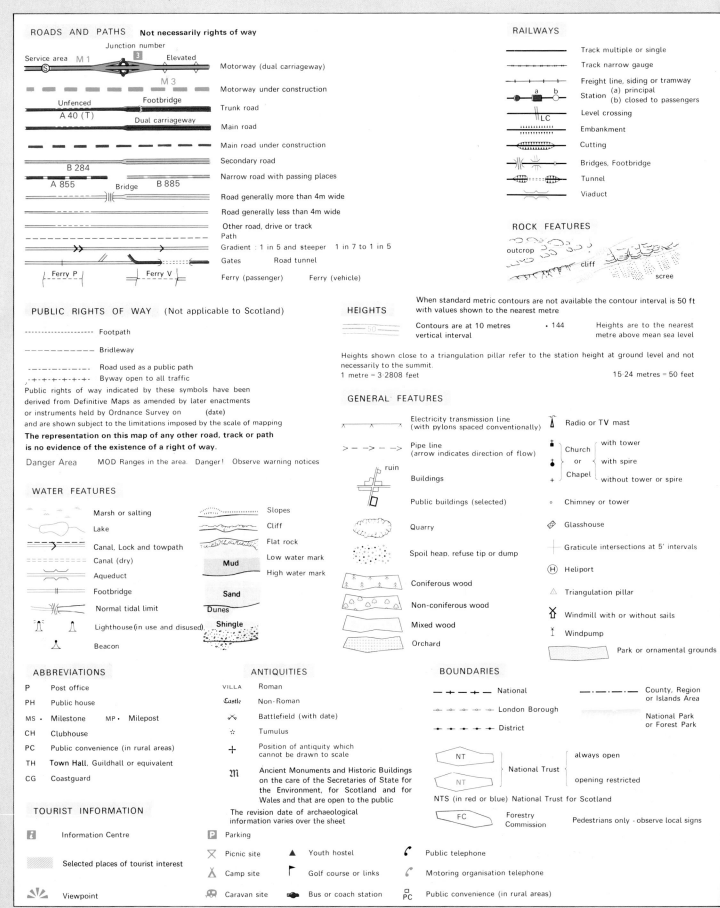

ROADS AND PATHS   Not necessarily rights of way

Service area M 1 Junction number 3 Elevated	Motorway (dual carriageway)
M 3	Motorway under construction
Unfenced Footbridge A 40 (T) Dual carriageway	Trunk road
	Main road
	Main road under construction
B 284	Secondary road
A 855 Bridge B 885	Narrow road with passing places
	Road generally more than 4m wide
	Road generally less than 4m wide
	Other road, drive or track
	Path
	Gradient : 1 in 5 and steeper 1 in 7 to 1 in 5
	Gates Road tunnel
Ferry P Ferry V	Ferry (passenger) Ferry (vehicle)

PUBLIC RIGHTS OF WAY   (Not applicable to Scotland)

.... Footpath

----------- Bridleway

-·-·-·-·-·- Road used as a public path

-+-+-+-+-+- Byway open to all traffic

Public rights of way indicated by these symbols have been derived from Definitive Maps as amended by later enactments or instruments held by Ordnance Survey on   (date) and are shown subject to the limitations imposed by the scale of mapping

The representation on this map of any other road, track or path is no evidence of the existence of a right of way.

Danger Area   MOD Ranges in the area. Danger! Observe warning notices

WATER FEATURES

	Marsh or salting		Slopes
	Lake		Cliff
	Canal, Lock and towpath		Flat rock
	Canal (dry)	Mud	Low water mark
	Aqueduct	Sand	High water mark
	Footbridge	Dunes	
	Normal tidal limit	Shingle	
	Lighthouse (in use and disused)		
	Beacon		

RAILWAYS

	Track multiple or single
	Track narrow gauge
	Freight line, siding or tramway
a b	Station (a) principal (b) closed to passengers
LC	Level crossing
	Embankment
	Cutting
	Bridges, Footbridge
	Tunnel
	Viaduct

ROCK FEATURES

outcrop
cliff
scree

HEIGHTS

When standard metric contours are not available the contour interval is 50 ft with values shown to the nearest metre

50	Contours are at 10 metres vertical interval	· 144 Heights are to the nearest metre above mean sea level

Heights shown close to a triangulation pillar refer to the station height at ground level and not necessarily to the summit.
1 metre = 3·2808 feet   15·24 metres = 50 feet

GENERAL FEATURES

	Electricity transmission line (with pylons spaced conventionally)		Radio or TV mast
	Pipe line (arrow indicates direction of flow)		Church or Chapel with tower
ruin	Buildings		with spire
	Public buildings (selected)		without tower or spire
	Quarry	○	Chimney or tower
	Spoil heap, refuse tip or dump		Glasshouse
	Coniferous wood		Graticule intersections at 5' intervals
	Non-coniferous wood	(H)	Heliport
	Mixed wood	△	Triangulation pillar
	Orchard		Windmill with or without sails
			Windpump
			Park or ornamental grounds

ABBREVIATIONS

P	Post office
PH	Public house
MS ·	Milestone MP · Milepost
CH	Clubhouse
PC	Public convenience (in rural areas)
TH	Town Hall, Guildhall or equivalent
CG	Coastguard

TOURIST INFORMATION

i	Information Centre
	Selected places of tourist interest
	Viewpoint

ANTIQUITIES

VILLA	Roman
Castle	Non-Roman
	Battlefield (with date)
☆	Tumulus
+	Position of antiquity which cannot be drawn to scale
m	Ancient Monuments and Historic Buildings on the care of the Secretaries of State for the Environment, for Scotland and for Wales and that are open to the public

The revision date of archaeological information varies over the sheet

P	Parking		
X	Picnic site	▲	Youth hostel
Λ	Camp site		Golf course or links
	Caravan site		Bus or coach station

BOUNDARIES

—+—+— National	—·—·— County, Region or Islands Area
—○—○—○— London Borough	National Park or Forest Park
—•—•—•— District	

NT / NT	National Trust always open / opening restricted

NTS (in red or blue) National Trust for Scotland

FC	Forestry Commission Pedestrians only - observe local signs

	Public telephone
	Motoring organisation telephone
PC	Public convenience (in rural areas)

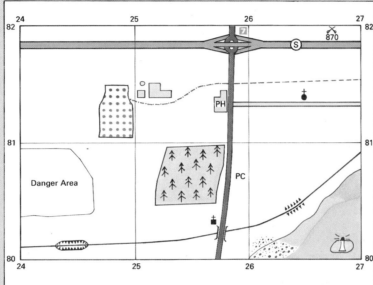

▷ Look carefully at the pictures.
Each one could have happened at only one place on the map.
▷ Use the conventional signs to identify where each scene took place.
▷ Copy and complete the chart.

Picture	Symbol	Grid ref.	Description of event
A		267,819	Battle fought here in 870
B	PC		
C		257,804	
D			
E			

31

Crossword grid

¹E	N	T	²R	A	N	C	⁴E
V			E				A
A		⁵S	I	X			T
⁶N	⁸E	S	T		⁷T	⁹V	
S	O			¹⁰M		¹¹I	N
	L			I		D	
¹²B	O	O	T	S		E	
				S		O	

Buried Treasure

Buried Treasure

1. Start at East Cowes.
   Go S along the A 3021.
   Pass Whippingham. At the
   roundabout turn E along the
   A 3054 through Ryde to Puckpool Point.   (Tin)

2. Travel S along the A 3055. Turn
   W at Sandown. Pass the caravan and
   camping spots at Branstone.   (Stone)

3. Continue on A 3056 to
   Blackwater. Turn S through
   Rookley. Stop at Godshill.   (Gold)

4. Go on along the A 3020.
   Pass the caravan and camp site.
   Turn S. at the crossroads on the
   B 3327. Stop before the golf course at
   Stenbury Down.   (Ruby)

To Dot and Randall

Ordnance Survey Maps reproduced with the permission of The Controller, Her Majesty's Stationery Office. Crown copyright reserved. Copyright 1988.

Published in 1991 by
CollinsEducational
An imprint of HarperCollins*Publishers*
77–85 Fulham Palace Road
Hammersmith
London W6 8JB

Reprinted in 1992

First published in 1988 by

Ordnance Survey and Holmes McDougall

Romsey Road   Allander House
Maybush   137/141 Leith Walk
Southampton   Edinburgh
SO9 4DH   EH6 8NS

Ordnance Survey ISBN 0 319 000 95 8
CollinsEducational ISBN 0 00 316 124 2

Printed by Canale Spa, Italy

Acknowledgements

Aerofilms
Linda Edmondson
Goad Plans Ltd.
Lake District National Park Authority
Liverpool Museums
John Mills Photography Ltd.
Penrith Mountain Rescue Team
David Williams

Design and illustration by Barrie Richardson